21ˢᵗ
Century
Skills Library

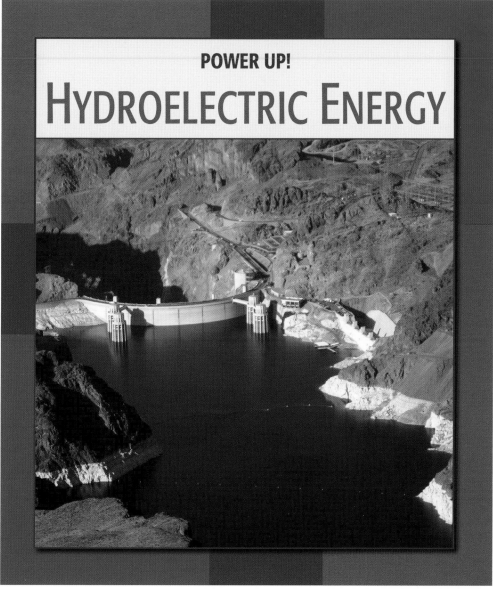

POWER UP!

HYDROELECTRIC ENERGY

Tamra Orr

Cherry Lake Publishing
Ann Arbor, Michigan

Published in the United States of America by Cherry Lake Publishing
Ann Arbor, MI
www.cherrylakepublishing.com

Photo Credits: Page 25, Photo Courtesy of United States Air Force, Photo by
Captain Gerardo Gonzalez

Library of Congress Cataloging-in-Publication Data
Orr, Tamra.
  Hydroelectric energy/by Tamra Orr.
      p. cm.—(Power up!)
    ISBN-13: 978-1-60279-049-0 (lib. bdg.)   978-1-60279-098-8 (pbk.)
    ISBN-10: 1-60279-049-3 (lib. bdg.)   1-60279-098-1 (pbk.)
  1. Hydroelectric power plants—Juvenile literature. I. Title. II. Series.
  TK1081.O765 2008
  621.31'2134—dc22   2007006234

*Cherry Lake Publishing would like to acknowledge the work of
The Partnership for 21st Century Skills.
Please visit www.21stcenturyskills.org for more information.*

TABLE OF CONTENTS

CHAPTER ONE

THE POWER OF WATER

Water is essential to all forms of life.

Water. It is one of the things that it is easy to just take for granted.

After all, you turn on the faucets, and there it is. You want a drink, a

bath, or a shower—no problem. Need to wash your car? Just get the hose.

Time to water the flowers in the garden? Grab the watering can.

Water is essential to all living creatures, from the smallest cell to the largest redwood and everything in between. This definitely includes humans! Along with helping keep the whole planet alive, water is also amazingly powerful. Humans have known that for thousands of years. For countless generations, they have used water to help them produce power to help them do jobs.

Through the Ages

For centuries, people used waterwheels to provide the power for needed jobs. Buckets of water poured regularly over paddles on the wheel to make it turn. These wheels were mainly used to grind

Learning & Innovation Skills

How much water did you use today? A toilet flush takes 5 gallons, a bath takes 40, and a 10-minute shower takes 25. Count up the ways you used water today and how many times you used it for each task. Then total up your one-day water use.

In many waterwheels, water pushed against blades in the wooden wheel to make it turn and thus produce energy.

flour and corn. They were an important part of almost every mill. Water wheels also ran equipment such as **lathes,** looms, and saw blades. In 1086, a list of all of the property in England at the time included more than 5,000 waterwheel-driven mills!

By the late 1800s, waterpower was being used to produce electricity. In 1878, a home in England was lit up through hydroelectricity, that is, electricity produced by the power of water. Two years later, Michigan's Wolverine

Chair Factory used lamps powered by water. The very first hydroelectric

power plant opened on the Fox River in Appleton, Wisconsin, on

September 30, 1882.

*In the 1800s, factories that wove fabric often used waterwheels
as the source of energy to operate the looms.*

By 1940, there were more than 3,000 hydroelectric plants throughout the world. Then the numbers decreased as other energy sources became more popular. By 1980, there were only about 1,400 hydroelectric plants.

However, the number has begun to grow again. Currently it is about 2,500. Today, hydroelectricity is one of the world's most widely used alternative energy sources and can be found in more than 100 countries on almost every continent.

CHAPTER TWO

THE GOOD SIDE OF
HYDROELECTRIC ENERGY

*Norris Dam in East Tennessee across the Clinch River has been
providing hydroelectric energy to the region since 1936.*

For the last one hundred years, nations around the world have produced large amounts of hydroelectric energy by building **dams**. These monumental projects have been among the largest structures ever built. They require millions and millions of dollars, many tons of material, and thousands of work hours to create. However, they have changed the lives of millions and millions of people for the better.

The TVA

Impossible as it may seem now, even in the 1930s, some parts of the United States did not have any electricity. One of these areas was the Tennessee Valley, which covers 80,000 square miles of the states of Tennessee, Alabama, Georgia, Mississippi, Kentucky, North Carolina, and Virginia. In 1933, President Franklin Roosevelt and Congress created the Tennessee Valley Authority (TVA) to help this poor economic region. One of its main jobs was to provide electricity.

Over time, the TVA built 29 hydroelectric dams. Along with several other sources of power, the TVA today distributes electricity to more than 150 local power companies through 17,000 miles of transmission lines. The TVA has improved the lives of millions of people in the region. Its low energy costs have brought jobs and prosperity to people in

Learning & Innovation Skills

The TVA's 17,000 miles of transmission lines would stretch more than two-thirds of the way around the world. Since the lines are in a relatively small geographic area, what does this tell you about the availability of electricity once the lines were all in place?

the area. For example, Japanese car manufacturer Nissan decided in 2006 to move its North American headquarters to the city of Nashville, Tennessee.

A Huge Project in Egypt

For more than 5,000 years, the Nile River has been the lifeblood of Egypt. It provided drinking water and transportation for the people. Its floods brought needed nourishment to nearby fields. All this is good. However, the unpredictability of the floods also brought disaster and death. In rainy years, heavy floods drowned people and animals. In dry years, the people and animals suffered from thirst. In the 1950s, the Egyptian government decided to do something.

*The Nile River has been home to a distinctive type of boat
called a felucca for many centuries.*

The government decided to build a huge dam that would control the

river. Called the Aswan High Dam, it was finished in 1970. It is made of

rock and clay and used 18 times the amount of material needed to build

the famous Great Pyramid near the Nile River at Cheops. The dam captures floodwater during rainy seasons and releases it during droughts. The dam also produces huge amounts of electricity, often delivering it to regions of Egypt that never had it before. The dam allowed 30 percent more land to be farmed. This in turn increased the economic prosperity of the people as well as their food supply.

Hydroelectricity in Brazil

The South American nation of Brazil today gets almost 85 percent of its electricity from hydroelectric plants. This amazing statistic ranks the nation among the world's top users of hydroelectric power. The

This interior photo of the Itaipu Dam shows its enormously strong cement walls and the huge machinery it contains.

huge Itaipu hydroelectric dam on the Paraná River is the core of this

power. The Itaipu Dam is the largest in the world. In fact, it has been called

one of the Seven Wonders of the Modern World.

The Itaipu Dam is gigantic. Building it even meant changing the course of the Paraná River. The dam is as tall as a 50-story building, and the amount of cement used would make 210 football stadiums. More than 50 tons (45 metric tons) of earth and rocks had to be moved to make way for the dam. The steel and iron needed would build 380 copies of the Eiffel Tower in Paris, France!

The Benefits of Hydroelectricity

Every year in the U.S., hydroelectric plants produce energy that is equivalent to 500 million barrels of oil. Worldwide, hydroelectric plants replace 22 billion gallons (83 billion liters) of oil or

*Hydroelectric dams have a great advantage in that the cost
of their fuel—water—probably will not go up as the
costs of coal, natural gas, and petroleum will.*

120 million tons (109 metric tons) of coal. Brazil's Itaipu Dam plant alone

creates electricity that would need 434,000 barrels of oil a day if oil were

used instead of waterpower. All of this is very good news because—unlike

oil—hydroelectricity is an infinite resource.

21st Century Content

The safe disposal of radioactive waste is a major problem around the world. Current American plans call for building an enormous storage facility under the desert in Nevada, but it will not be ready for use until 2017. The Yucca Mountain facility has employed more than 1,000 people in its construction and covers 1,150 acres (4.7 km²).

Hydroelectricity has many other advantages. It uses water, which is both plentiful and free. No fuel is burned, so no air pollution is created. Unlike fossil fuel plants, hydroelectric plants do not emit carbon dioxide or sulfur dioxide into the air. There are no waste products or radioactive contaminants to deal with as in nuclear energy. Nor are there mines or wells to dig as with coal and oil.

Hydroelectric energy is far more reliable than wind, solar, or tidal power, which are often affected by weather. Hydroelectric plants also can be brought to full power quickly when the demand suddenly increases. Hydroelectric dams often create large lakes

The creation of hydroelectric dams has also created water recreation areas in Kentucky, Nevada, Washington, and many other states.

that can have many **recreational** uses. Fans of fishing, boating, swimming,

and other water sports often appreciate hydroelectric dams for the

opportunities they provide.

CHAPTER THREE

NOTHING IS PERFECT

*Bonneville Dam on the Columbia River now has "salmon ladders"
to allow the fish to migrate up river as they used to.*

As wonderful and simple as hydroelectricity may sound, there are

problems with this energy source. One problem is the amount of water,

money, and land they require. Another problem is what they do to the

environment. America's Hoover Dam was built in the 1930s and today supplies electricity to customers in Arizona, Nevada, and California.

However, if it were built today, the dam might have problems getting the OK.

Fish can be killed in the blades of the dam's **turbines,** which must turn to

produce electricity. Interfering with a river's flow can create cold and warm

layers, too. Since a cold layer loses most of its oxygen, fish cannot survive in

it. Dams may also interfere with

migration routes. Dams on the

Columbia River in Washington

state have special "fish ladders"

to help salmon move up the river

as they need to.

The huge lakes that many

dams create can also bury useful

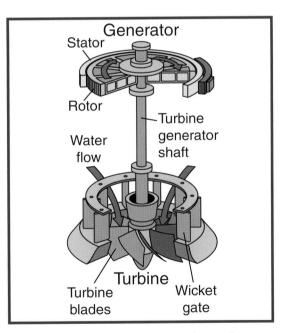

Turbines are enormous pieces of machinery, as the drawing with a person beside it shows.

and important things. For example, valuable mineral resources may be buried, along with farmland that has been productive for many decades.

Important archeological sites may also be endangered. Egypt's gigantic Temple of Abu Simbel was one. The temple is more than 3,300 years old and is one of the masterpieces of ancient Egypt. To keep it from being destroyed by dam construction, many groups got together and laboriously cut the stone temple into sections and moved it to the top of a nearby hill, where it sits today. It took $80 million and four years of work.

Sometimes, these lakes cause the **displacement** of millions of people. This is what happened with China's enormous Three Gorges Dam on the Yangtze

River. The Yangtze is the longest river in Asia and the third longest river in the world. Building the dam meant that almost two million people lost their homes, jobs, and everything else. Experts estimate that about four million people annually lose their homes due to construction of new dams worldwide. The electric power may help many in a region, but it can definitely hurt some people, too.

A major crack appeared in China's Three Gorges Dam in 2000, several years before the dam was even completed.

CHAPTER FOUR

THE FUTURE OF HYDROELECTRIC POWER

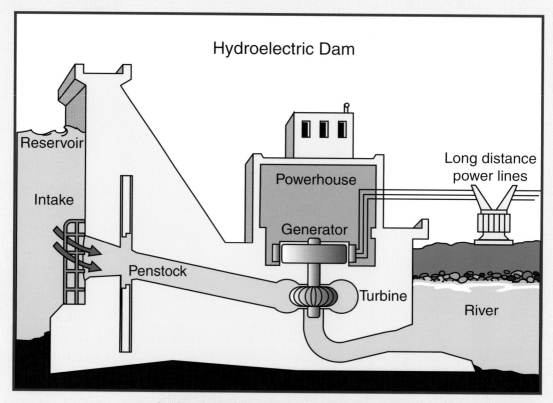

Hydroelectric Dam

Reservoir

Intake

Penstock

Powerhouse

Generator

Turbine

River

Long distance power lines

Hydroelectric dams must be incredibly sturdy and are built to last a century or more.

There are many future possibilities for hydroelectric power. Only about 13 percent of worldwide potential currently is being used.

However, experts do not believe hydroelectric power will ever reach its full potential for two reasons. One reason is construction costs, which often run to multiple millions of dollars.

A second reason is the growing awareness of such plants' negative environmental impact.

Thinking Small

What does the future hold for hydropower? No one is quite sure. Experts are now looking at ways to keep harnessing this power but without damaging the environment or disrupting people's lives. One way to do this

Micro hydroelectric plants can be small enough to power just a single home.

Even small streams can be used to create hydroelectric energy.

is through the installation of so-called micro hydroelectric plants. These are much smaller plants that produce only five megawatts of electricity or less. There are already more than 100,000 micro plants just in the nation of China.

Although these smaller hydroelectric plants are not nearly as powerful, they are often still able to provide sufficient electricity for local villages and industries. Some of these plants do not ever require the construction of a new facility. Instead, they are attached to existing water works, so the cost and environmental impact are far less.

Micro hydroelectric systems have worked out well in Nepal, Peru, Sri Lanka, and Kenya. They are called "run of the river" systems because they do not require a dam. Instead, they simply divert water from a local stream or river. The water is channeled into a valley and then dropped into a turbine. This system has many possibilities, especially for countries that are struggling to provide affordable power for their citizens.

21st Century Content

Nepal is a small nation in Asia among tall mountains, including Mt. Everest, the tallest mountain in the world. Nepal is one of the poorest countries in the world, too. Usually such mountainous terrain is a big hindrance, but when it comes to hydroelectricity, it is a great asset. The supply of reliable but inexpensive electricity has allowed people in Nepal to establish new businesses and increase productivity in existing ones.

Some of the world's tallest waterfalls such as those in Norway,
Canada, Peru, New Zealand, South Africa, and the
United States are being tapped for hydroelectric energy.

Water is truly an essential part of life. By harnessing its power and availability, many areas of the world have electricity. It is a clean and renewable source, but it does not come without its costs. Water is a source that the world will continue to turn to for energy, but not without thinking carefully about any environmental effects first.

The micro hydroelectric systems in Nepal, Peru, Sri Lanka, and Kenya are built on streams in the mountains. Why is that the ideal location for a micro hydroelectric system?

Glossary

accumulation (uh-kyoo-myuh-LEY-shuhn) gathering into one place

dams (damz) barriers constructed across waterways to control the flow or raise the level of water

displacement (dis-PLEYS-muhnt) act of removing or relocating to another place

flow (floh) to move along in a stream

lathes (leythz) machines for shaping a piece of material, such as wood or metal, by rotating it rapidly along its axis while pressing a fixed cutting or abrading tool against it

recreational (rek-ree-EY-shuhn-ul) pastime, diversion, exercise, or other resource affording relaxation and enjoyment

reservoir (REZ-er-vwahr) natural or artificial place where water is collected and stored for use

spawning (SPAWN-eng) process of procreation for fish and other marine creatures

turbine (TUR-bin) machines having a rotor, usually with vanes or blades, driven by the pressure, momentum, or reactive thrust of a moving fluid, such as steam, water, hot gases, or air

FOR MORE INFORMATION

Books

Adams, Richard C, et al. *Energy Projects for Young Scientists.* New York: Franklin Watts, 2003.

Draper, Allison S. *Hydropower of the Future: New Ways of Turning Water into Energy.* New York: Rosen Publishing, 2003.

Goodman, Polly. *Water Power.* London: Hodder Wayland, 2005.

Graham, Ian. *Water Power.* London: Hodder Wayland, 2001.

Oxlade, Chris. *Water Power.* North Mankato, MN: Stargazer Books, 2006.

Peterson, Christine. *Water Power.* New York: Children's Press, 2004.

Webster, Christine. *Water Power.* New York: Weigl Publishers, 2005.

Other Media

Learn more about the famous Hoover Dam at *http://www.pbs.org/wgbh/amex/hoover/*

To find out more about how a hydroelectric dam works, go to *http://www.wvic.com/hydro-works.htm*

Another good source for basic information about hydroelectricity is *http://www.energyquest.ca.gov/ask_quester/answers_hydro.html*

INDEX

ABOUT THE AUTHOR

Tamra Orr is a full-time writer and author living in the gorgeous Pacific Northwest. She loves her job because she learns more about the world every single day and then turns that information into pop quizzes for her patient and tolerant children (ages 16, 13, and 10). She has written more than 80 nonfiction books for people of all ages, so she never runs out of material and is sure she'd be a champion on *Jeopardy!*